"The beauty of animals lies in the diversity of colors and the exuberance of their forms."

Rozana Sarmanho

2024

This Book Belongs to:

Test Color Page

Congratulations on completing this coloring book! Remember that creativity and artistic expression are important for mental and emotional well-being. Keep coloring and exploring new forms of creative expression.

www.ingramcontent.com/pod-product-compliance
Lightning Source LLC
Chambersburg PA
CBHW080937260726
48661CB00010B/3963